T R E E S,

V A L L E Y S

and

V I S I O N S

by

Iris Grenfell

MOORLEY'S Print & Publishing

ISBN 0 86071 475 6

MOORLEY'S Print & Publishing

23 Park Rd., Ilkeston, Derbys DE7 5DA
Tel/Fax: (0115) 932 0643

CONTENTS

PART 1

TREES

Page

PART 2

VALLEYS & VISIONS

SYNOPSIS

T R E E S

1. THE TREES OF CHOICE - GENESIS 2:15-17 - Adam & Eve made their choice - how do we make ours?

2. THE TREE OF WISDOM - JUDGES 4/5 - Deborah, the woman who 'kept her cool'

3. THE TREE OF DEPRESSION - 1 KINGS 19:1-8 - Elijah. What brings on depression - how do we deal with it?

4. THE TREE OF RESENTMENT - JONAH - Jonah learns that God's ways are not our ways.

5. THE TREE OF OPPORTUNITY - LUKE 19:1-10 - Zaccheus made the most of his opportunity - do we?

6. THE TREE OF HEALING - EXODUS 15:22-27 - Israel in the wilderness; see a picture of things to come when the bitter waters were healed.

7. THE TREE OF DELIGHT - SONG OF SOLOMON 2:3-5 - The maiden shows us the way into relationship and communion with the Lord.

8. THE TREE OF REDEMPTION - DEUTERONOMY 21:18-21 [ACTS 5:30-31] [Galatians 3:13 and 1 Peter 2:24]

VALLEYS & VISIONS

1. THE VALLEY OF VISION - ISAIAH 22 - A disturbing vision becomes a glorious vision - prophetic of Christ.

2. THE VALLEY OF BACA - PSALM 84 - Dryness into refreshment

3. THE VALLEY OF DELIVERANCE - JOSHUA 10:1-14 - Is anything too hard for the Lord.
   THE VALLEY OF GIANTS - JOSHUA 15:8; 18:16 Dealing with the 'giants' in our lives - Fear, Unbelief Bitterness, Unforgiveness etc.

4. THE VALLEY OF DOUBT & DESPAIR - JEREMIAH 33 - Finding God in captivity.

5. THE VALLEY OF DECISION - JOEL chapter 3 - Life's most important decision.

6. THE VALLEY OF DISAPPOINTMENT - ACTS 16 - Don't let disappointment lead to discouragement - God does not make mistakes.

7. THE VALLEY OF BERACHAH - 2 CHRONICLES 20 - Obedience brings the Victory.

8. THE VALLEY OF RESTORATION - EZEKIEL 37:1-14 Ezekiel's vision of restoration and revival and its relevance today.

9. THE VALLEY OF THE SHADOW OF DEATH - PSALM 23:4 The Light in the Valley.

THE TREES OF CHOICE

GENESIS 2:15-17

How careful we have to be when making choices! A wrong choice can have far reaching consequences, as the first people on earth discovered.

God gave one simple command - Do not eat of the fruit of the Tree of the Knowledge of Good and Evil - but with this command He never took away their freedom of choice as to whether to obey it. However, He did warn Adam and Eve that IF they chose to eat of it, they would 'surely die', i.e. spiritually, for we know they did not die physically when they DID eat from it.

They could have eaten from any other tree in the paradise which God had given them, including, presumably, the Tree of LIFE [Genesis 2:8-9]. However, they made their own choices [Genesis 3:1-24], and, as a result, became separated from God, whose companionship they had enjoyed until then [Genesis 3:8].

It is important to notice the things that made Eve and then Adam choose to disobey God's command, and we can learn an important lesson from it.

I JOHN 2:16 helps us here:-
"For all that is in the world - the LUST OF THE FLESH, THE LUST OF THE EYES and the PRIDE OF LIFE is not of the Father, but is of the world".
See how Eve succumbed to these:-
"The woman SAW that the tree was GOOD FOR FOOD... and that it was PLEASANT TO THE EYES..."
[The Lust of the Flesh and the Lust of the Eyes - Genesis 3:6].
"...And a tree to be desired to MAKE ONE WISE ..."
The serpent had said, 'In the day you eat it your eyes
shall be opened and you shall be as gods knowing good
and evil' Genesis 3:5].

The tragedy and deception was that they would know GOOD without being able to do good, and they would know EVIL without being able to stop being and doing evil [See Romans 5:12-19].

We should be careful, then, as to what motivates our choices. Do we eat of the Tree of the Knowledge of Good and Evil, or do we eat of the Tree of LIFE - which is a picture of Christ - and so have the LIGHT OF LIFE?

In the Eternal state, there is no mention of the Tree of the Knowledge of Good and Evil, but the TREE OF LIFE is still there, bringing blessing to ALL [Revelation 22:1-7]. THE CHOICE IS OURS!

THE TREE OF WISDOM

JUDGES chs.4-5

"And Deborah, a prophetess, the wife of Lapidoth, she judged Israel at that time, and she dwelt under the palm tree of Deborah between Ramah and Bethel under Mount Ephraim, and the children of Israel came up to her for judgement".

Here is a very interesting instance in the recorded history of Israel. In amongst the list of all the men who judged and delivered Israel, we read of Deborah the wife of Lapidoth.

She was a prophetess in her own right - one who, according to Matthew Henry was 'instructed in Divine Knowledge by the inspiration of the Spirit of God - she judged Israel as God's mouth to them [for a prophet is a spokesman for and of God]'.

Deborah seems to have had a calm and clear spirit. She dwelt under the PALM TREE and the people came to her. The Palm Tree was between Ramah [meaning 'the Height'] and Bethel [meaning 'House of God'], and this would immediately convey the thought of a person who maintained her life with God, living above the ordinary level, in communion with God, and who maintained her own peace and rest - a person who, amid the stress and strife and dire emergencies of her time, 'kept her cool'! She dwelt in the shade, at rest, and therefore was able to give clear sound instruction in a crisis, as taught by the spirit of God. She was also able to rise up and give strength and encouragement to the one who SHOULD have been Israel's leader and she was one who was esteemed and heavily relied upon, because Barak would not go to battle unless Deborah went with him [Judges 4:8].

This was truly a woman's war, for according to Deborah's prophecy [Judges 4:9], the Lord used a home-maker named Jael to deliver Israel from her dreaded enemy Sisera [Judges 4:17-22].

Deborah's calm, restful spirit not only enabled her to deal wisely in judgement, and to deal with a national emergency, but resulted in great creativity as she sang a song inspired by the Spirit Who recorded the incident for us to read about today [Judges 5].

Had Deborah lived in New Testament times, her verse might well have been 'I will sing with the Spirit, I will sing with the understanding also' [See 2 Corinthians 14:15(b)].

Let us then seek out our own particular Palm Tree, where we can rest in what God has done in Jesus Christ for us, where we can hold communion with Him and where we can hear from the Holy Spirit those things that will give us Wisdom, Direction, Holy Energy and Creativity in Worship.

THE TREE OF DEPRESSION

1 KINGS 19:1-8

I'm sure we have all, at one time or another, and for varying reasons, found ourselves sitting under the Tree of Depression. What had brought Elijah to this place where he sat dejected, utterly cast down and longing to die? Hadn't he recently won a great victory over evil in the Name of His God? [1 Kings ch. 18]. Hadn't the land now been blessed with rain after the three-and-a-half year drought he had prayed for and of which he had prophesied? [See 1 Kings 17:1; 18:1; James 5:17-18]. YES, but now things were different - the prophet who had stood alone against 800 false prophets, now fled from an angry vindictive queen who swore to take his life.

Fear was the main factor in Elijah's depressed state, and fear is still a big factor in depression today. Elijah had good cause to fear you might say, but if we are honest, most of us are like Winston Churchill who said, "I fear thousands of things, most of which haven't happened yet!" And there lies the key - our fear is usually over the consequences of the past, or not knowing what is to come.

Other factors contributed to Elijah's low state. He had had an exceptionally demanding time - he was obviously extremely tired because the Angel found him asleep and woke him and later said to him, 'The journey is too great for you' [v.7.] He also felt alone and not appreciated as he mentioned later. He had obviously neglected himself in performing his ministry to others - he needed food and drink and God KNEW this and provided it for him. When his strength returned, he was able to go on refreshed and renewed.

Simple factors like Elijah's lack of proper sleep, diet, etc., can contribute to a low state, but we don't need to sit under the JUNIPER TREE. As a minister once said to a young christian man, "You need to chop down your Juniper Tree".

We need to see that we get proper rest and refreshment in our service for the Lord, but, above all, we need that spiritual refreshment that comes straight from Heaven. When Jesus told His disciples to 'Come apart and rest awhile' [Mark 6:31], it was because they were over-busy and 'there were many coming and going', and they were to be apart from the crowds, but TOGETHER WITH JESUS.

Our 'coming apart' should not be with ourselves under the Juniper Tree, but with Jesus the Bread and the Water of Life. Sometimes we need to 'come apart for a while' to save us from coming apart altogether!

If we 'come apart' with Jesus, we shall find He is sufficient for our needs and we shall be able to go on in the strength He provides.

THE TREE OF RESENTMENT

JONAH CHAPTER 4

Here is a tree under which we can, perhaps unwittingly, find ourselves sitting. JONAH had come out of his disciplinary experience in the whale's belly and he was obedient, as last, in preaching to the people of Nineveh, giving them God's warning of utter destruction if they did not repent. His preaching had the effect of causing the whole city, from the King down to the youngest subject, to repent publicly. This, however, did not actually please Jonah as one would have expected, rather we are told that he was 'exceedingly displeased and very angry' [Jonah 4:1] - he was so cut up he even wanted to die!

Was it because now God was getting the glory because of Nineveh's repentance instead of Jonah because of his prophecy of destruction? It is almost too incredulous to think of Jonah going out of the city and sitting under a gourd to see if God would REALLY spare them after all!

Perhaps there was an element of disbelief in God's Word which had clouded his judgement at that time - Jonah's Jewishness and his personal convictions got in the way of his being glad at God honouring His own Word.

Jonah very much resented the happy, relieved state of the Ninevites - weren't they Israel's Gentile arch-enemy? Why should they be spared? According to Jonah, Salvation was not only of the Lord, but only for the Jews!

God showed him his pettiness by allowing a worm to destroy the gourd which had given him shade and now it was the heat that made Jonah want to die. God showed Jonah that he had more thought for the life of a gourd [which had given him shade] than for hundreds of thousands of Ninevites who could have perished -60,000 of which were young children.

What is our reaction when people whom we, perhaps, consider to be unworthy and past redemption receive forgiveness and a new life from Christ? Are we pleased when the newly saved join our church, or when backsliders are restored? There is a New Testament counterpart to Jonah found in the parable of the lost son in Luke 15. The Elder brother was not at all pleased when his sinful, but repentant, brother returned home - he didn't think he deserved all that rejoicing and welcome from their father - he was bitterly resentful that his own obedience and faithfulness was apparently unnoticed. It can be like that with us and we need to remember the words of the father to the Elder son:- "You are always with me and ALL THAT IS MINE IS YOURS" [Luke 15:31].

May we heed the words of the Apostle Paul to the Ephesians:"Let all bitterness and indignation, wrath [passion, rage and bad temper] and resentment [anger, animosity] ... be banished from you with all malice, spite, ill-will or baseness of any kind and become useful and helpful and kind to one another, tenderhearted, compassionate, understanding, loving-hearted, forgiving one another readily and freely as God in Christ forgave you" [Ephesians 4:30 AMP. Bible].

THE TREE OF OPPORTUNITY

LUKE 19:1-10

I wonder how good we are at seizing opportunities? Do we RECOGNIZE opportunities when they come our way? And if we do, what do we do about them?

Zaccheus, of whom we read in LUKE 19, is a good example of someone who saw an opportunity, acted on what he saw, and got much more than he ever expected as a result.

Zaccheus has always struck me as being quite a sad little man. We are told that he was shorter than average [Luke 19:5] and maybe he resented this all his life. He would not have been popular within his own community because he worked for the Romans - as what in World War II we would have called a collaborator. Then in his role of Tax Collector, he would have been even less popular, particularly as we deduce from the story that he was a CORRUPT Tax Collector [19:8], and to crown it all, he was a CHIEF Tax Collector which probably made him disliked by those under his supervision. Zaccheus had certainly grasped the opportunity to become rich! However, when he knew that Jesus was on a walk-about in his city [Jericho], he took the opportunity of seeing Him by climbing into a sycamore tree where, he thought, he would have a good view and remain unseen. We are not told WHY he wanted to see Jesus, perhaps he had heard that there was a former tax collector among His disciples, [Matthew 9:9], but something must have motivated this self-made man to do so - something other than financial gain, of which Jesus must have been aware, for He stopped at the tree and called Zaccheus by name telling him to "Come down" for He, Jesus, wanted to visit him in his home.

We know that the outcome of Zaccheus climbing the tree of opportunity was that he came into a personal knowledge of the Son of God and received a personal salvation [19:9] which resulted in a changed life.

Zaccheus was SAVED in the true sense of the word - he was saved from the wastage of a useless selfish life, he was saved from the defeat of the power of his own sinful lust of money and prestige, because now he wanted to restore, with interest, the money he had taken by fraud. Now he wanted to help those less fortunate than himself instead of 'feathering his own nest'. Now he was saved from the eternal consequences of the Law he had broken and he had come into the security of the family of God through God's Son Jesus Christ, and into the forgiveness which He brought. In that way he became a true 'son of Abraham'.

Have we taken the opportunity to meet with Jesus? Are our hearts open when God's Word tells us of Him as it is read or preached? Do we listen to the testimony of those who belong to Him? Have we taken the opportunity to be saved from eternal spiritual danger, to be saved from a useless life, to be kept from defeat and to become secure in God's forgiving love?

Then, too, do we take the opportunities that come our way to speak to someone else about Him, and do we take the opportunities of putting wrongs right and of doing good to those less fortunate? Let US be quick to climb the Tree of Opportunity.

THE TREE OF HEALING

EXODUS 15:22-27

Here we read of one of the trials the nation of Israel faced when in the wilderness. They had come out of the slavery of Egypt, they had known deliverance from Pharaoh at the miraculous Red Sea crossing, but now they were in the wilderness. One day they would enter the Promised Land of Canaan and enjoy all it produced, but between Egypt and Canaan came the wilderness and it was to be a place of trial and testing and proving God.

This particular trial was over one of the ordinary commodities of life - WATER - and after three days in the wilderness, they had not found any, and even when they did find water at Marah they could not drink it because it was bitter. Then they began to complain and worry and blame their leader Moses.

We can find a parallel in the Christian life when reading this account of Israel's experiences. We, as christians, can know we have been delivered from our 'Egypt' [sin] and we have been brought out from servitude to a hard taskmaster [satan] by the protection of the Blood of the Lamb of God - Jesus Christ - Whose Blood cleanses from all sin. We have crossed our 'Red Sea' and left behind our past life. However, we, too, have 'wilderness' trials and testings.

Just as with Israel, the wilderness trials show us ourselves and test our characters, but they also show us our God. Too often the trial is over some ordinary, everyday thing and we complain and murmur and blame. We go through a dry patch spiritually and it is easy to murmur against our leaders, and worry ourselves into an anxiety state. When we DO find what we think we are looking for it often leaves bitterness.

Moses cried to God on behalf of the people and God showed him a tree which Moses cast into the bitter waters and which had the effect of making the water sweet and pleasant to drink. The tree that healed the waters at Marah [meaning "bitter"] is a type of the Lord Jesus Christ who can sweeten any bitter situation. When He comes into a life by invitation, that life becomes sweet, but in order for that to be the case, He had to be cast into the "bitter waters" of death on our behalf.

Let us remember in our trials that complaining will not remedy the situation, but let us use the circumstances as an opportunity to draw more of the sweetness and Grace of the Lord Jesus as we call upon Him.

At this point in their history God affirmed His covenant with Israel as His Special people. He revealed to them one of His Covenant Names - JEHOVAH RAPHA - "I AM THE LORD THAT HEALETH THEE" [Exodus 15:26]. He is still the same today to those who have entered into the New Covenant with Him, through His Son Jesus.

Interestingly, the next stop for Israel was Elim, a place of 12 wells and 70 Palm Trees and by this we know that the wilderness is not ALL trials and coming through a 'wilderness trial' is often followed by being brought into a place of abundance.

Let us learn to trust in our time of trial and testing the One who came that we might have Life and have it MORE ABUNDANTLY.

Elim was a sample of the plenty that Israel would experience in Canaan. The 'more abundant' life that we have by the Holy Spirit here is only a foretaste of the perfection and plenty that we shall experience in the Heaven to come.

THE TREE OF DELIGHT

SONG OF SOLOMON 2:3-5

This tree is found in one of the most beautiful books in the Bible. The Song of Solomon - or Song of Songs - is a book which not only portrays the beauty of the deepest, most intimate human relationships, but speaks of the relationship between Christ and the believer.

Scholars tell us that the book may be looked at in three ways:-

a) A portrait of God and Israel

b) A portrait of Christ and the Church

c) A portrait of Christ and the Believer

and it is to the last of these I refer.

The maiden is speaking and she says:-

"As the Apple Tree among the trees of the wood, so is my Beloved among the sons of men" [2:3].

She is saying that this tree, which is different and bears good fruit, is right there in the wood amongst all the other trees, where one would not really expect to find it. The Apple Tree mentioned here has been identified with the Quince or Mandrake and one would perhaps expect to find it in an orchard or a garden. We can think of our Lord Jesus Who did not remain in the Heavenly setting to which He belonged, but Who came to earth and took on human flesh. HE stood out from other men because of HIS fruit which was an obedient, sinless life.

Men could see Him, hear Him, touch Him - He was in every way made like them, living right in their world and doing the same things daily - yet He stood out like the Apple Tree amongst the trees of the wood.

Today He is still in the world by His Holy Spirit and He still stands out. By faith He can be seen, heard and touched. Unless our eyes are really blinded, it is not difficult to recognize an apple tree among the trees of the wood, and unless we are really spiritually blinded, it is not difficult to recognize Jesus among the sons of men.

"No mortal can with Him compare
Among the sons of men
Fairer is He than all the fair
That fill the Heavenly train"

Like the maiden in the Song of Solomon, we can all have an Apple Tree experience. The maiden said:- "I sat down under His shadow with great delight and His fruit was sweet to my taste."
' She knew the benefits of that tree being in the wood. "I sat down..." she voluntarily, confidently adopted the position of rest it offered.

We can sit down and rest when we know Jesus, for He has promised that those who are weary and heavy-laden shall be given rest, and those who are desirous of learning from Him will find even more rest. [Matthew 11:28-29]. When we are willing to rest from all that is US and come to Him not standing (in our own ability), nor walking, nor running, but seated (sat still or 'dwelling'), we shall find out exactly WHERE we are seated. We shall find that we are, in fact, "seated in Him in Heavenly places" [Ephesians 2:7].

"Under His shadow..." - Here is Protection!

[Shadow (Tsel) means a 'shade' or 'defence'] and when we adopt this attitude of rest under a tree we are shaded from the heat of the sun, sheltered from wind and rain and perhaps hidden from view by the overhanging branches.

We get the same kind of protection from the Lord Jesus, we can know His coolness and shade in times of stress and over-activity, His protection from the heat of trials or distress, His defence against those things that would seek to harm us in our souls and spirits. As Isaiah says:-

"A MAN shall be as a hiding place from the wind
and a covert from the tempest, as the shadow
of a great rock in a weary land" [Isaiah 32:3].

"With great delight ..." this was an active experience and it was one that was sought after ["delight" (chamad) means "desire"]. She

WANTED to be there - there was no 'take it or leave it' attitude, no 'might as well' approach, it was with GREAT DESIRE that she sat down under the shadow of the tree. That is why her experience became such a full one. I suppose she could have sat there along with others and mildly enjoyed the time, but to her it was personal, vital and special.

'I SAT DOWN UNDER His shadow with **GREAT DELIGHT** [DESIRE]. How is our approach to the Lord Jesus? Do we get the 'fringe benefits' of being in His Presence with others as just the thing to do, or do we, even IF with others, seek Him personally with eagerness? It is often inconvenient and costly to do this. What about day-by-day? Do we seek Him out when we are alone, do we know the 'Apple Tree' fellowship on a one-to-one basis?

"His fruit was sweet to my taste" - The fruit of any tree carries in it ALL that the tree is. If I eat an apple, I am tasting all of the energies, processes and ingredients of the apple tree which have gone into producing the fruit.

To sit under the apple tree is to be within easy reach of its fruit. I suppose someone could have picked an apple and brought it to her, but that wouldn't be the same as reaching out taking for herself, straight off the tree - no staleness or damage then.

Apples belong to that group of foods which help to prevent infection. The maiden found out that the fruit was sweet to her taste - it fed, refreshed and delighted her, and protected her. Just so, as we are seated in Christ and are desirous of all that He can be to us, we can be fed, refreshed and satisfied with ALL that He is, for all that He is will then be readily available to us. We shall 'taste and see that the Lord is good'.

Love is always a two-way experience or it cannot be a totally fulfilled relationship. Love is the spontaneous outgoing of all that one is towards another, the desiring to know and to share completely with the other. Where this is on both sides, there is true love. It may be expressed in different ways on different levels, but basically that's what it is. Or look at it this way - there is an initiator who is outgoing towards the loved one, the loved one responds and returns his/her love, so then is the initiator to the other one - Love begets Love - and so it grows and deepens and multiplies.

The Beloved had been the initiator because He was there in all that he was, typified by the apple tree - branches outstretched, rest and protection, fruit and refreshment readily available - the maiden willingly and spontaneously came and sat and desired and partook.

So it is with the Lord Jesus - in the greatest message of Love this world has ever known, He stretched out His arms to mankind on the cross of Calvary offering genuine, unselfish, protective and, therefore, satisfying LOVE - ours for the taking!

The girl in the Song greatly desired and partook and in return found a deeper and more wonderful expression of Love and knew a fuller experience of it. So as we willingly partake of ALL that the Lord Jesus offers by His expression of Love on the cross, we are led into depth and fulness of ALMIGHTY LOVE.

"He brought me into the Banqueting House..."

Her delight in Him caused Him to bring her into deeper depths and higher heights. "He brought ME..." the Lord Himself conducts us to the place we may see typified in the Banqueting House. We cannot go there without Him, we CAN only go there because of Him!

It speaks of a royal place - ordinary people don't banquet! Yet she says, "He brought ME into the Banqueting House." It was a wonder to her, and what a wonder to us when we realize that we sinners, who were cut off from God by our sin, have not only been forgiven, but have been brought into the very Presence of God and "accepted IN the Beloved One". It is a place of status such as the world could never give us - we are acceptable to GOD. The Banqueting House was a place of 'pressed out wine' [yayin]. Here we don't just get the fruit but the absolute end product - the fulfilment of all that was in the tree.

When we are willing to enter our relationship with the Lord Jesus and go on in it with Him, we truly drink 'the royal wine of Heaven'. During His earthly life Jesus had changed ordinary water into wonderful wine at a wedding in Cana. Banquets often occur at weddings don't they? A love relationship between a boy and a girl moves towards a wedding and the two enter into covenant and, forsaking all others, are joined in the closest of human ties. As our love-relationship with Jesus deepens, we realize we have entered into covenant with Him, we are joined by a tie greater than anything on earth. As we commit ourselves to Him in this covenant, we find that the ordinary water of human life has become the wonderful wine of a spiritual life - and we are in the Banqueting House. In order that we could drink to the fullest of all that He is, He was crushed and trodden like grapes in a vat. When He suffered on the cross, out flowed the rich pure wine for us to share. This is not any cheap 'duty free' - this is the real thing - the vintage that improves with age and never goes sour or does us harm.

"His banner over me was love" [Banner or Standard (degel)]. "I am under His ensign - I am secure for He owns me and is showing to everyone that He has and will undertake all that concerns me".

Can't you just imagine the maiden thinking this in joyous amazement?

It is precisely so with the Lord Jesus, Love is the standard He lifts up over us. This is the place where there is no fear, the place where we may know that which passes human knowledge.

What is the response from the girl to this deeper experience of love? She is overwhelmed, "I am sick of love" - in other words, "It's too much, this love is making my head swim", yet she longs to know more.

"Stay me with flagons", "stay" meaning to 'support' or 'establish'; 'Flagons' (ashishah) are little cakes of grapes. "Support and establish me on the same things I've been tasting and enjoying - the wine that comes from the fruit. From now on I want this to support me and make me strong". "Comfort (raphad) - support me with Apples" - "I won't forget where it all started and when the wine is too much for me I shall be supported by the Apples and the Flagons".

Do we experience Christ and taste of Him and enter into a wonderful experience with Him and then run away satisfied with that experience? I fear many of us do and we fail to be supported and built up and established. The Apple Tree experience and the Banquet experience are not 'once for all' experiences that we must look back on with regret. If we have become neglectful and dry and our experience seems empty, if we have left our first love or if we have allowed ourselves to get over-wearied and frustrated, we can always visit the Apple Tree. We can always just sit there and let the shade and rest and refreshing do us good. We shall soon find ourselves in the Banqueting House.

24

THE TREE OF REDEMPTION

Scripture, in several places, speaks of the cross on which Jesus died as a 'Tree' and there is a specific reason for this.

When Peter and other Apostles were arrested by the Jewish Council for disobeying their command not to preach or teach in the Name of Jesus, nor even about the Name of Jesus, they said this:-

> *"We must obey God rather than men. The God of our forefathers raised up Jesus Whom you killed by hanging Him on a tree"* [ACTS 5:30-31].

The use of the word 'tree' rather than cross would have been very significant to the Jewish Elders and their minds would have, undoubtedly, gone to what their Law said about those who were hanged on a tree.

DEUTERONOMY 21:18-21 tells of the usual punishment for wrong-doing such as adultery, drunkenness, gluttony, disobedience to parents, which was stoning to death. However, if the person had committed a particularly heinous crime, he was to be hanged on a tree until sunset. This more severe punishment was not only to cleanse out the evil from the community, as with stoning, but it signified that the person was cursed by God.

Peter was telling the Jewish leaders that although they regarded Jesus as having been cursed by God, this had been disproved when God raised Him up and exalted Him [Acts 5:30-31].

"However," says Paul in his Epistle to the Galatians [chapter 3:13] "Jesus Christ did become cursed, but not His own account - the curse He bore on the tree was ours". Because we cannot keep God's Laws, we find ourselves cursed by it - the list of all the sins that make us cursed are in Deuteronomy chapter 27 and they include things like taking bribes, being unkind to blind people, oppressing widows and orphans and sexual immorality. The good news, however, is that:

> *"Christ purchased our freedom, redeeming us from the curse of the Law's condemnation, BECOMING A CURSE FOR US, for it is written 'Cursed is everyone who hangs on a tree'* [Galatians 3:13 AMP. Bible].

The cross of Calvary was a TREE OF REDEMPTION for us though it was a tree of shame and curse for Jesus.

Peter, in his Epistle says:

> *"He personally bore our sins in His own body on the TREE and offered Himself on it that we might cease to sin and live to righteousness. By His wounds you have been healed"* [1 PETER 2:24 AMP.Bible].

Have you received the fruit of the Tree of Redemption? Have you believed the sacrifice that Jesus Christ made for you - have you believed that He became a CURSE for YOU that YOU MAY BE MADE RIGHT WITH GOD?

Have you received the forgiveness and healing for sin that this offering obtained for all of us?

Have you received the LIFE that comes to us as a result of God accepting that offering on our behalf, by raising Jesus up to a place of exaltation and by pouring out His Holy Spirit on those that believe? [See ACTS 2:32-33; ACTS 5:30-32].

All this Grace can be ours when we receive the finished work of Jesus Christ, God's Son, which He accomplished on the TREE OF REDEMPTION.

VALLEYS and VISIONS

"Valleys and Visions go together" was a statement I read recently in a book by Warren Wiersbe ['Be Comforted'], and on looking into the scriptures, I found it to be true. The enemies of Israel once told them that their God was only a "God of the hills" and not "God of the valleys" [1 Kings chapter 20:21-28]. On that occasion the Israelites proved the Syrians to be quite wrong, even though they had filled the whole country and Israel's camps looked like two little flocks of kids amongst them [v.27], because Syria suffered a terrible defeat that day after a prophet had told the King of Israel that their God would give them victory.

There are experiences recorded in scripture, both of the nation and of individuals who had 'valley' experiences, and of how God brought them through and gave them a renewed vision. Some of these experiences occurred in actual geographical valleys, others in 'valley' situations.

THE VALLEY OF VISION

Isaiah was once in a place that was called 'the valley of vision' [Isaiah Ch:22] and there he had an understanding of what God thought of His own people who were, apparently, unrecognizable from the pagan nations around because of their unbelief and sinful rebellion [22:1-14].

Isaiah saw the outcome of their behaviour - they would be besieged by enemies, they would die from famine and disease and all their self-effort would not help them. Their leaders were concerned only with self-advancement and were no example to the people in returning in repentance to seek God's help. One of them, Shebna, was deposed and replaced by Eliakim a man of God's choice, whom He called 'My servant'. Here Isaiah's vision extends from his own day to the day when Jesus Christ would come as God's Perfect Servant on earth. The words used about Eliakim [Isaiah 22:22] are used about the Lord Jesus in Revelation 3:7:

"These things saith He that is Holy, He that is true,
He that has the key of David, He that opens and no
man shuts, and shuts and no man opens".

When we come into Salvation through Jesus, Who is the Door [John 10:9] no one can shut it against us, conversely if we neglect to come into His Salvation, we find that the door is shut and no man can open it to us. Eliakim was also described as 'a nail in a sure place' and this is a type of the God's Servant Jesus, who is absolutely dependable and everything to do with our soul's security may confidently hang on Him.

The 'valley' of a disturbing vision, became the valley of a prophetic, glorious vision and so can many of the 'valley' experiences in our lives. Even if we read the prophecies of the end of those who reject God's Servant, let us also take note of all the promises of God which are fulfilled in Him, and may we be encouraged to steer others into the kingdom through the DOOR- Jesus Christ.

THE VALLEY OF BACA

PSALM 84

Psalm 84 is a Psalm of Peace and speaks of the pilgrimages to the Tabernacle and the unity and fellowship of God's people as they journeyed together to the special place at times of worship.

Anyone barred from this congregational time of fellowship would have mourned the fact as we see perhaps from verse 2. This verse describes the inner heart condition of such a person, and perhaps we can identify with this feeling as we contemplate the worship of God together with His people. Some need to be encouraged, uplifted, exhorted or urged, but the person in verse 2 had a healthy appetite for the things of God, and to have a heavenly appetite is a great blessing .

Then in verse 6 we read of the Valley of Baca and we get the sense of refreshment even in the dreariest part of the way. The word 'BACA', according to scholars, got its name either from 'Bacal meaning a mulberry tree, which would flourish on dry ground, or from 'Bochim' which means 'Tears or Weepings'. Bochim was the name given to the place where God's people were rebuked by an angel for their disobedience to God [Judges 2:1-5] and so it became the 'Valley of Weepings'. However, the psalm says that the Valley of Baca becomes a WELL. Even though God's people passed through dry valleys and wept, they had GOD for their refreshment - He was the source or well from which they drank and were refreshed and strengthened.

No dry experience can be so great that to the trusting heart God will not make it a WELL - a place of 'drawing forth' that which is needed whether it be cleansing, repentance, sustenance or growth. Even if that well should seem to dry up, we read that "the rain also filleth the pools", and so in our experience, however dry it gets, God will send the rain to fill the pools and we shall go from strength to strength. Our God is the God of the Valley of Baca - He is the SAME God in all our weepings and dryness.

Then in the Psalm the writer has a vision of God as a 'sun and a shield', the One who not only gives Grace, but Glory. We, too, can often have a new revelation of God's love after being in the 'valley of weepings'. The warmth of His love will soothe, comfort and soften us, which is so necessary since trials make us either bitter or better. We realize that He is our spiritual defence and protection when we are low, and He not only gives us undeserved love, but shares with us, through Jesus Christ, His Glory!

Trusting Him during our time in the valley of Baca will cause us to know that 'No good thing will He withhold from them that walk uprightly'.

THE VALLEY OF DELIVERANCE

JOSHUA 10:1-14

'Valley' experiences were usually to do with deliverance and restoration. Joshua and Israel found themselves in deep trouble in the valley of Ajalon where they faced an onslaught from five kings and their armies who were assembled against them. The Lord gave His word that Joshua would win against the enemy, and, strengthened by this, Joshua became very bold. He commanded the sun and the moon to stand still in order that Israel would have enough time in daylight to combat their enemy, and that the sun would be in a good position for them to do so. Strengthened and believing in God's Word, Joshua saw God as the One with Whom he was in partnership - the One he could approach with holy boldness, and the One in Whose Name he could do great exploits!

We, too, may find the odds very much against us at times and we may need a help that is extra-ordinary. We can find it in the same God and by the same means. We can be strengthened by trusting in His promises, we can ask the question which Abraham was asked by the Lord - 'Is anything too hard for the Lord?' [Genesis 18:14]. As we are strengthened, we find we can 'come boldly to the throne of Grace to obtain mercy and find Grace to help IN TIME OF NEED'. There we shall find a supply of the Holy Spirit which will help us to overcome all opposition and do the seemingly impossible in His Name. The valley of Ajalon became, for Joshua, the valley of deliverance - it can be the same for us.

THE VALLEY OF GIANTS

[JOSHUA 15:8; 18:16]

This valley was said to be the place where the descendants of the 'giants' mentioned in Genesis 6:4 had lived -- Og, King of Bashan being one of the last [Joshua 12:4]. There are, however, many things which can come into our lives and appear as 'giants' to us, but we can find that God is the God of this 'valley' too.

"GIANT FEAR" is mentioned in Hebrews 2:15 where it speaks of those who 'through fear of death were all their lifetime subject to bondage'. Jesus has delivered us from the Law of sin and death and we need not fear it any more if we trust in Him, because He came to give us LIFE, and after physical death we need not fear the judgement of God because Jesus was judged for our sin on the cross of Calvary. If the Son has set us free then we are free indeed.

UNBELIEF can often seem as a 'giant' and keep us in a gloomy valley experience. Mark 6:24 speaks of a man who wanted to believe but had just a little doubt - he did the sensible thing and confessed it and asked Jesus to help him with it.

BITTERNESS, according to Hebrews 12:15 can take root in a person and if it is allowed to spring up in them, not only the person, but many others are defiled as a result. This can be a great 'giant' but God can help us have victory over it and can replace it with the positive good fruit of His Holy Spirit.

Another great 'giant' which can rob us of joy and blessing is UNFORGIVENESS. Ephesians 4:32 tells us to 'Be Kind, tenderhearted, forgiving one another as God, for Christ's sake has forgiven you'.

When we look at the example of Jesus in Forgiveness, surely all that we could hold against others fades into insignificance. The Lord will give us the needed Grace to forgive others, for if we do not have forgiveness for others, neither will the good of God's forgiveness be ours. Let us look to the God of this particular 'valley' for help.

Other 'giants' stalk and ruin our experience such as jealousy, envy, pride, but God can be the God of ALL.

THE VALLEY OF DOUBT & DESPAIR

[JEREMIAH 33]

Jeremiah was a faithful prophet of God even though it meant proclaiming an unpopular message. God's people were to be punished for their continued sin and rebellion against Him in spite of His repeated warnings through the prophets.

Jeremiah was given the task of telling the people that they would be overcome by the Chaldeans, their holy city would be destroyed and they themselves, together with King Zedekiah, would be taken into captivity until they repented [32:1-5].

Jeremiah had been arrested and put into prison in the King's house and one wonders what his feelings would have been at that time. Did he doubt at all? Did he begin to despair? He couldn't have felt much like a prophet there in prison, and yet in that 'valley' in his life God gave him a prophetic word twice.

It was there in prison that Jeremiah was enabled to see God as the One who could speak to and reach His people through ALL circumstances. Jeremiah's vision of God was renewed - he saw Him once more as the Creator and Sustainer of all things [33:21]. He was the God who would hear and answer the cry of His people and He was the God who gave HOPE for the future. 'Call unto Me and I will answer thee and show thee great and mighty things which thou knowest not' [33:3], and God went on to say how He would, in love, restore the people to their own land after their time of punishment by exile.

During his prison sentence, Jeremiah received God's promise of the coming Messiah, whom He called 'The Branch of Righteousness'. He was to come out of the family of King David, and God would fulfil His promises to David by sending Him [33:15-26]. God assured Jeremiah that His promises were certain and sure and could be utterly relied upon.

Many modern day Christians who have been imprisoned for their faith can testify that Jeremiah's God has not changed and that He visits His faithful ones, affirming Who He is and giving hope for the future of the world through Christ.

We may never find ourselves in such a state, but should we ever be brought into a situation where we may be open to doubt and despair because we have faithfully given God's word, then we, too, will find that as we call, He answers and He will assure us of Who He is and give us HOPE through Christ for the future.

He is the God who comes to us in all our valleys.

THE VALLEY OF DECISION

JOEL chapter 3

'Multitudes, multitudes in the valley of decision! For the Day of the Lord is near in the Valley of Decision' [v.14].

The valley referred to by Joel in chapter 3:14 was actually the valley of Jehoshaphat. It was the place where the nations were to be assembled for the judgement of God [3:2] which will be in relation to the attitudes they have had towards His special people Israel. 'I will plead with them there for My people...'[3:2]. God announced His intention of restoring His people as He ended their years of captivity.

However, Joel's prophecy had a much more far-reaching application, for he spoke of a coming day when there would be a final judgement on earth - the Day of the Lord. The happenings of that 'Day' are described vividly by Joel throughout the book [1:15; 2:30-31; 3:15] and are re-iterated by Peter in his sermon on the day of Pentecost [Acts 2:19-20]. It was to be preceded by an outpouring of God's Holy Spirit and would result in great deliverance for those who would 'call upon the Name of the Lord' [Joel 2:32; Acts 2:21]. This, of course, was partially fulfilled on the day of Pentecost when the Holy Spirit came to earth to remain [Acts 2:16] but the complete fulfilment of the prophecy is yet to come.

During this proclamation Joel spoke of the 'valley of decision' and said that there were multitudes in it. It was 'make your mind up time' for those living in the shadow of such terrible coming judgement. We today are obviously much nearer to that time, and world conditions would bear this out if studied together with the Old Testament prophecies and the teachings of Jesus.

Thankfully the picture was not all black, for Joel went on to describe the blessings his own people would enjoy as his vision was enlarged. We, as Christians, see a parallel in this book with the Church. We are all at sometime in our lives in the 'valley of decision' - we have to decide whether we will take God's appointed way of salvation, Jesus Christ, and whether we will 'call upon His Name' i.e. to trust Him as the only saviour from sin and the only means of us becoming part of God's special spiritual people the Church.

Our decision on that point will determine God's decision in judgement. Since Jesus Christ, God's Son, bore ALL the judgement for ALL sin on the cross of Calvary, we will not be required to be judged for them again if we have accepted His sacrifice on our behalf. We shall enjoy the blessings of a redeemed and delivered people.

The 'fountain which shall come forth of the house of the Lord' [3:18] is a type of Christ, who causes us to be cleansed, refreshed, renewed and fruitful.

Whatever circumstance has caused us to have a 'valley experience' the answer is the same - we must 'call upon the Name of the Lord', but the most important decision, in the light of coming judgement, is to 'call on Him and be SAVED'.

THE VALLEY OF DISAPPOINTMENT

[ACTS 16]

The Apostle Paul faced another 'giant' with whom a meeting can be very lowering. In fact this is one of Satan's prime agents, for 'giant' disappointment often leads to discouragement. The great 19th Century preacher, C.H. Spurgeon, tells the story of a preacher who dreamed the devil was giving him a guided tour of hell. Satan showed him all the weapons he had used to triumph over Christians down through the ages and they included such things as persecution, doubt, famine, warfare, trials, and at last they came to a table where something was covered over. "This," said Satan, "is my greatest weapon. This has caused more Christians to turn back than anything else".

Lifting off the cover he revealed a table with a single notice on it, and on the notice was only one word - DISCOURAGEMENT. The preacher woke and from that day his ministry was never the same, for he determined not to let disappointment get him down to the point where he got discouraged and felt like giving up.

It is good to know that even people like the Apostle Paul experienced disappointment, but instead of becoming discouraged he waited on God and received a glorious new vision.

After he had been through Galatia, Paul's own plan was to continue spreading the Gospel in Asia, but the Holy Spirit did not allow this [Acts 16:6]. Not deterred, Paul went through Mysia and tried to go into Bythinia which bordered the Black Sea, but once again the Holy Spirit checked him. This could have resulted in severe disappointment and discouragement for Paul but he continued on to the coastal city of Troas [Acts 16:6-8]. That night - there in the valley of disappointment - Paul had a vision in which he saw a Macedonian man who asked him to come to his country and help them. The man was recognizable as a Macedonian and the message was short and clear. Instead of the valley of disappointment, a fertile field lay before him and Paul knew beyond all doubt that this was the Lord's direction [Acts 16:9-12].

The interesting thing is that Paul's first convert in Philippi was

Lydia - a lady who originally came from Thyatira, which is in Asia, where Paul had been forbidden to go by the Holy Spirit, [Acts 16:14-15]. A church DID spring up in Thyatira anyway and it is mentioned in Revelation 1:11.

Life is full of disappointments and we are often in that particular 'valley'. People, even leaders, let us down, circumstances won't work out, even the weather seems to be a hindrance sometimes, our bodies become older and we are restricted in things we once did, but if we maintain our trust in the Lord at these times and realize 'our times are in His hand' we will not slip into discouragement, but we will be able to quietly wait on Him. Then we are in a position to have a real vision of what He wants for us and from us and our witness will then be far more effective than our own plans would have allowed.

"They that wait upon the Lord shall renew their strength. They shall mount up with wings as the eagle, they shall run and not be weary, they shall walk and not faint" [Is.40:31]. "My soul wait thou only upon God, for my expectation, hope, and the thing that I long for is from Him" [Psalm 62:5].

THE VALLEY OF BERACHAH

[2 CHRONICLES 20]

The name 'Berachah' was given to a valley after the people of Judah had seen the Lord deliver them from their enemies in a most marvellous way. 'Berachah means 'Blessing' and so this valley was very aptly named.

Judah and their King Jehoshaphat were attacked by the Moabites and Ammonites together. Jehoshaphat wisely set himself to know the mind of God for His people and he proclaimed a day of fasting, he himself leading the people in prayer. His prayer began with his reminding God of Who He was in their eyes, and what He had done for them in the past, and then he told God of the awful situation they were in and asked for His help [2 Chronicles 20:1-13]. In answer to this prayer, the Spirit of God caused one of the Levites to prophesy that GOD would give them victory and that if they ordered themselves in the way He commanded, they would not even need to fight! The King and congregation accepted this inspired directive and worshipped and praised God [v.14-19]. Their faith was put into obedient action and they assembled themselves in their proper order as Jehoshaphat exhorted and encouraged them. In an act of faith, Jehoshaphat ordered the singers - not the fighting men - to lead the people and they were to 'Praise the beauty of holiness and Praise the Lord for His mercy endures forever' [2 Chronicles 20:21].

As they were obedient, the LORD dealt with the enemies who suffered complete loss and the spoils of war greatly enriched Judah. It was then that the people assembled in the valley, which they named BERACHAH, to give thanks to the Lord before triumphantly returning to Jerusalem [v.22-30].

We, as God's people, come into blessing in the same kind of ways. As we give ourselves to prayer and learn how to pray both in private and in church life, God answers with the Holy Spirit. It is while we set aside everything else and come to God on a specific matter that we often receive His direction. We can take a pattern from Jehoshaphat if we are not skilled in praying.

It is good to remind God of Who He is in our eyes, what He has done for us and to put before Him the situations and people about which we want to pray in simple, straightforward terms. We can tell God everything - He knows already, but He wants us to tell Him - and we will never take Him by surprise nor shock Him.

As we are obedient to the way He leads us, and as we believe and act on His word, we find that He will undertake for all our situations. Then, even before it actually happens, we can worship and praise Him with hearts that believe for the victory. That way we are brought into the 'valley of blessing' where our experience and vision of Him is enlarged and we are encouraged to trust Him in future.

"The blessing of the Lord - it makes me rich..." Proverbs 10:22.

THE VALLEY OF RESTORATION

[EZEKIEL 37:1-14]

The prophet Ezekiel was taken, by the Spirit of God, to a valley which was full of dry bones and there he had a vision of the power of God to create and re-create. We know that only God can give real life to make a person a living being [Genesis 2:7], whilst men may make images and likenesses, only GOD can give the BREATH OF LIFE. Similarly, no man or other power could make those dead, dry bones live again, for they had once been people who had lived and moved and had being.

Scripture tells us the bones were 'very dry' which indicates that they had been in that condition for a long time, and we can see the two things which were necessary in order for them to have real life again:

1) THE WORD OF THE LORD - God told Ezekiel, "Prophesy unto these bones and say unto them 'O ye dry bones HEAR THE WORD OF THE LORD'" [v.2].

2) THE SPIRIT OF GOD - God promised, "I will cause breath to enter into you and you shall live" [v.5].

Ezekiel prophesied as the Lord commanded, but when the bones and sinews came together and flesh came upon the bones, and skin covered the flesh, they had a form of life but no REAL life - they were now the "living dead". Ezekiel had to prophesy to the wind - a type of the Holy Spirit - [John 3:6 & 8] and when the BREATH OF GOD entered the forms of the people they became ALIVE and STOOD and became a PEOPLE OF POWER, "an exceeding great army".

Ezekiel interpreted this vision to the people as a picture of what God would do with His people. He would "resurrect" them as a people and bring them to their own land even "out of your graves". They had ceased to be known as a nation being as good as dead in their captivity, but by being given real life from God, they would once again be marked out as His own people in their own land.

He did it after the Holocaust of World War II - the state of Israel was established in 1948 and are now an "exceeding great army".

God can do the same in the spiritual sense for believers, for an apostate church, and He will do the same for the believing church at the coming of Jesus [John 5:25-26; 1 Thessalonians 4: 13-18].

As far as the individual is concerned, God has given us human life, but it is not until we have the Breath of the Holy Spirit that we have real spiritual life. We are born again by the Spirit of God acting upon the Word of God as we have believed its record of Jesus [See 1 Peter 1:23; James 1:18; John 1:11-13; John 3:1-16].

If an individual Christian, or a church becomes dry in its experience, then as the Word of God is received, believed and obeyed, God will answer with the breath of His Holy Spirit and bring restoration, revival and powerful effective witness .

"Spirit of the Living God, fall afresh on me".

THE VALLEY OF THE SHADOW OF DEATH

PSALM 23:4

In this 'Shepherd' Psalm David speaks of the Valley of the Shadow of death, realising that all humans must eventually pass through it. However, He has a vision in his heart of the true and faithful Shepherd who will not leave him there alone but who will go through it with him - "I will fear no evil for THOU ART WITH ME," he says. We can take this promise for ourselves when our time comes to pass through that particular valley, but we can also take it in relation to the shadows which come into our experience in life's trials. In 'Pilgrim's Progress' John Bunyan puts the Valley of the Shadow of Death much earlier in the Christian's life than the crossing of the last river into the Celestial City [which speaks of his going to be with the Lord].

David describes the valley as the 'valley of the SHADOW of death' not the 'valley of death'. It is ONLY a shadow and everyone knows that to have a shadow, there must be LIGHT around somewhere. The LIGHT is of course, Jesus the Lord who has promised to be with us always and never leave us. We have His Light when we have been pressed, oppressed and depressed - when our spirits have been in the valley of the shadow of death, we have lived on in spite of it. C.H. Spurgeon describes this kind of experience as one with "wild thoughts, mysterious horror and terrible depression" yet he says, "The Lord has sustained me" and this can be the experience of every believer in such times as it is realised that Jesus is going through it WITH them.

When it comes to the last great human experience of dying, we may have the same assurance. We can have Light in our 'valley of the shadow of death' if we have the Light of the World - Jesus - in our experience now. He has taken the fear out of death because He has done away with what makes death a thing to be feared - He bore the judgement for our sin on the cross and therefore we need fear no judgement from God after our own departure. The Light which we have in our lives through knowing Him personally as Saviour and Lord, will remain when we come to walk through this valley. Let us thank God for His abiding presence with us throughout life and even in the valley of the shadow of death.

> "He will keep me 'til the River
> Rolls its waters at my feet,
> Then He'll bear me safely over
> Where with loved ones I shall meet
> Yes, I'll sing the wondrous story
> Of the Christ who died for me
> Sing it with the saints in glory
> Gathered by the crystal sea".

NOTES:-

Scripture references taken from the Authorised King James Version except where stated otherwise.
Name meanings from Young's Analytical Concordance.
Quotations from hymns - Redemption Hymnal.
Other quotations from "Be Comforted" by Warren Wiersbe, and "Cheque Book of the Bank of Faith" by C.H Spurgeon.

MOORLEY'S

are growing Publishers, adding several new titles to our list each year. We also undertake private publications and commissioned works.

Our range of publications
includes: **Books of Verse**
Devotional Poetry
Recitations
Drama
Bible Plays
Sketches
Nativity Plays
Passiontide Plays
Easter Plays
Demonstrations
Resource Books
Assembly Material
Songs & Musicals
Children's Addresses
Prayers & Graces
Daily Readings
Books for Speakers
Activity Books
Quizzes
Puzzles
Painting Books
Daily Readings
Church Stationery
Notice Books
Cradle Rolls
Hymn Board Numbers

Please send a S.A.E. (approx 9" x 6") for the current catalogue or consult your local Christian Bookshop who should stock or be able to order our titles.